THE TRUTH

About

FEAR

God's Assurance of Help and Strength

in Times of Adversity

Mary Taylor Whitfield

Presented to: _____

By: _____

Date: _____

Occasion: _____

Personal Note:
_____
_____
_____
_____
_____
_____
_____
_____
_____

© 2002 by Mary Taylor Whitfield

Cathier Press
P.O. Box 763
Lizella, GA. 31052

Cover Design-Clarence Carner

Page Layout-Kevin Pou

ISBN-0-9720445-0-7

All rights reserved. No part of this publication may be reproduced or transmitted in any form or by any means without written permission of the publisher.

Scripture taken from the HOLY BIBLE, NEW INTERNATIONAL VERSION. Copyright © 1973, 1978, 1984 International Bible Society. Used by permission of Zondervan Bible Publishers.

The Thomases,

God has blessed us to share many experiences. Aren't we glad that His ways are so wonderful and purposeful? Let us continue to grow in faith and love.

Mary T Whitfield
5/11/02

Peace!

Dedication

I dedicate this devotional in memory of Etta Washington Cullers. She set a high standard of trusting God enough to embrace life in the face of death and promoted wholeness for women in the midst of her own illness.

Acknowledgements

George Espy, Jr. warrants a special tribute for editing and encouraging me to publish this work. At different stages of the writing, Etta Cullers, Sharon Childs, Cynthia Starr, Oceola Adams, Krysta Solomon and Ruby Dudley waded through pages of the rough draft to spot the errors of my mind and fingers. You were a great help.

I express special gratitude to my pastor, Eddie D. Smith, Sr., who contributed so much to this work by consistently teaching me how to study and apply God's Word. Also I thank God for James, my supportive husband, Kellise and Krysta, my loving children, and my kind family and friends. You are great armorbearers for all the Lord gives me to do.

Bless all of you!!!

Foreword

Over the past five years, Etta Louise Washington and I became associates, friends and co-facilitators for the Women of Color Breast Cancer Support Group which held its first meeting in January, 1996. Etta and I spoke often about our primary goal of educating women about the importance of prevention or early detection of this disease.

Until the end, Etta's faith was never shaken despite seeing this dreadful disease claim the life of her sister two years before her diagnosis. In fact, she often described her sister's death as "preparation for what I was to encounter in my own health." Through her initial diagnosis, recurrence and metastasis, she used her faith to overcome fear, ministering to others, and praising God regardless of her "lot."

It was through this type of Christian fellowship that Etta and Mary Taylor Whitfield (minister, orator, teacher, playwright) became friends. They each believed that God was their rock and that they could do anything through Him. They individually and collectively found ways to minister to the masses about the goodness and mercy of the Lord.

I have been very fortunate to be able to know, share and to work with each of these women. Therefore, it came as no surprise when Mary felt it "not robbery" to dedicate this, her first book, to Etta Louise Washington Cullers.

Dr. Shirley Marshall Black, Founder

Introduction

Have you ever read anything so simple yet powerful that you could hardly put it down? Did you want everyone else to read it too? This is what happened to me when I first grasped the simple truth in Isaiah 41:10. It was as if someone had handed me the key to one of the major riddles of life. In a way, God had. He simply told me what I could do and believe to be victorious in my daily walk. When I realized how effective this scripture could be as a weapon against fear, I quickly hid it in my heart. Others will say that it was on my tongue, too, for I began to share it with many people who were also in need of a spiritual boost. My role as a mother/wife/educator/church teacher/minister/friend and confidant to untold numbers gave me a vast clientele. Eventually, as I expanded my reading to other verses in the chapter, I found even more strength in those added words of comfort. Much later, I realized the importance of writing about the relief and solace I received in the simple, yet powerful, Word of God.

One particular person comes to mind when I think of the many people who have thanked me for sharing this scripture with them. Her name is Etta Cullers. From the first day of Etta's visit to the doctor, when a mysterious knot appeared in her armpit, to the time near the end of her life, we shared in communion about the miraculous power of God to help and strengthen. As the cancer ravaged her body, but not her indomitable spirit, she demonstrated a "fear not" attitude. At various stages of her illness, she told me of her reliance on the hope of Isaiah 41:10. The clear evidence of her peace of mind was displayed in her beautiful face as well as her determination to educate women about breast cancer. Hence, she organized a local cancer support group and raised thousands of dollars for research. After I completed the first revision of *The Simple Truth About Fear* in the summer of 1999, I asked her, along with another friend, to read it and make suggestions for changes. Her comment that the devotional was especially uplifting to her encouraged me to pursue its publication. Sadly, I allowed my other responsibilities to keep me from concentrating on the completion of the booklet. Thus she died as a strong warrior of faith before it was printed. Because of her reliance on the Lord in the face of illness and death, and the comfort in knowing that Isaiah 41:10 was a source of strength to her, I thought "it not robbery" to dedicate *The Simple Truth About Fear* to my friend Etta Washington Cullers.

My main focus in this devotional is to show how God responds to His people in a time of need, and how His people can be assured of His deliverance. The simple beauty of Isaiah 41 rivals Psalm 23 as a source of comfort and consolation. The average reader, not having to struggle to interpret Isaiah 41, can easily grasp what must be done to defeat the monsters of dread and doubt.

It is worthwhile for historical purposes to see the desperate condition of the Jews in chapters 1-39, along with the retribution for the nations that God used to discipline His people. Israel, once under the blanket of God's total protection, is now in exile. It is also noteworthy to see how God used a heathen nation under the leadership of Cyrus to chasten His people, but did not allow Cyrus to utterly destroy the nation of Israel. God's memory is long; in fact, it is as long as from everlasting-to-everlasting. He had not forgotten His promise to Abraham to continue to number his descendants. Out of that promise and His great love for His people, God spoke through Isaiah to restore confidence to a nation fallen from grace, calling them back under His wings of salvation.

Therefore, Isaiah 41 is a classic study in overcoming fear. The wretched condition of the Hebrew nation is much like our wretched condition today. We have become a backsliding nation, full of pride and poor relations with God. Weaker nations have taken our inheritance and used it for their glory. Our peace in the Lord has been broken by a restlessness caused by greed and the class struggle. The increase in serious illnesses such as cancer, heart disease and communicable diseases add even more fear. We are in captivity to ourselves, to debt, to our jobs and other responsibilities, and we are frightened of the consequences. Of late, terrorism has become a real threat as we witness more and more atrocious attacks on our country. We need a Word from the Lord. Isaiah can speak to us today.

Isaiah 41:10-18

So do not fear, for I am with you;
do not be dismayed, for I am your God.
I will strengthen you and help you;
I will uphold you with my
righteous hand.
All who rage against you
will surely be ashamed and disgraced;
those who oppose you will be as nothing and perish.
Though you search for your enemies, you will not find them.
Those who wage war against you
will be as nothing at all.
For I am the Lord, your God,
who takes hold of your right hand
and says to you,
Do not fear;
I will help you.
Do not be afraid, O worm Jacob,
O little Israel,
for I myself will help you," declares the Lord,
your Redeemer, the Holy One of Israel.
"See, I will make you into a threshing sledge,
new and sharp, with many teeth.
You will thresh the mountains and crush them,
and reduce the hills to chaff.
You will winnow them,

the wind will pick them up,
and a gale will blow them away.
But you will rejoice in the Lord
and glory in the Holy One of Israel.
"The poor and needy search for water, but there is none;
their tongues are parched with thirst.
But I the Lord will answer them:
I, the God of Israel, will not forsake them.
I will make rivers flow on barren heights,
and springs within the valleys.
I will turn the desert into pools of water,
and the parched ground into springs.

I WILL

Help

Strengthen

Uphold.

FEAR NOT!

DO NOT FEAR.
Isaiah 41:10

Those who know and trust God are the recipients of the blessings of assurance of protection and deliverance. Promises directed to a particular people at a particular time in the Old or New Testament are still available to you and me. As we read through God's Word, we can see the universality of His assurance: "*I am your God. You are my people.*" These words may have been spoken directly to the Jews, but when God inspired the writers of the Holy Word to pen His story, He spoke through them to the hearts of every believer. The church, that living body of baptized believers in Christ Jesus, can rest on those same promises of protection and blessings.

Despite the often repeated promises, we, the followers of Christ, have failed to fully grasp and act on the "fear nots" in the scriptures. Crossing over from fear to faith in the power of God today resembles the journey of the Jews from Egypt to the Promised Land. We struggle against the wisdom of man and the plague of doubts. We experience despair, do desperate things, and, in the end, make desperate pleas for help. Sometimes, we trust God enough to start the journey. However, we begin to lose our confidence once we encounter minor difficulties. Sadly, we may even turn around, failing to exercise the faith we already have. Why? Why? Why? The answer to this question is not always simple. One fact is obvious though: we fear the unknown, the hardship, the obstacles or even the opposition more than we fear the loss of God's favor.

Acting in fear is like walking on sinking sand. You're going somewhere but not in the right direction.

DO NOT BE DISMAYED.
Isaiah 41:10

God, a gracious and generous benefactor, has given believers in Christ the power to overcome fear. This awesome power comes through our position as joint heirs with Christ. Through Him we were adopted into the family of Abraham. When we come to understand that the struggles and deliverance of the Hebrew nation are applicable to our own struggles and deliverance, we can find hope for our dilemmas. If we believe that God constantly intervened on behalf of Abraham's descendants, why can't we have the assurance that He will do the same for us? Our inadequacies become His opportunities. Our weaknesses become His strengths. Our pleas lead to His response. Our spiritual walk is lighter because we are not terrorized by the "wiles of the devil." Additionally, we have the Holy Spirit dwelling in us, interceding on our behalf with Jesus, our great Advocate. Fear is overshadowed by faith. We are lifted up by the promises of God.

Imagine the fear of the children of Israel in the face of captivity by the Assyrians around 735 B. C., and later by the Babylonians. They lost faith as Isaiah prophesied doom and destruction. Highly favored at one time as the chosen of God, they were subject to foreign rulers. Isaiah probably surprised them when he began to repeat words of comfort. Imagine their shock since he had spoken of doom and destruction for so long. God's promise to still help, strengthen and uphold them in spite of their sins was like a breath of fresh air. Isaiah's powerful chapters of assurance can do for us what his words did for the Jews: **point us to God in all of our trials, give us hope, and show us that He will rescue us.**

Using the central focus of Isaiah 41:10-18, we will explore the unequivocal assurances given to the children of Israel, and use these simple yet powerful words to teach us in these latter days the simple truth about overcoming fear according to God's wisdom.

Prayer for Power and Protection

Lord, I render praises for Your might, majesty and awesome power. You always provide special favors for the children of faith. How blessed we are! The more we remain rooted and grounded in You the more we can expect protection and peace. You are so awesome! Even when we turn from You, Your chastisement is for our good. You then wait patiently to hear our prayers of repentance and open Your arms to restore us. If we were not assured of this fact, we would be lost in our fear, frets and failures.

Continue to remind me to give praise for Your power and protection. Teach me to surrender to You in all of my ways. Help me to learn to surrender my nagging doubts and feeling of inadequacies. Assist me in learning to trust the simple truths about overcoming fear. Please remind me often that You will help me, strengthen me and uphold me. Do it with Your powerful hand and with Your righteousness. I pray in the name of Your Son Jesus. Amen.

Do you also need to pray for power and protection?

So do not fear, for I am with you; do not be dismayed, for I am your God. I will strengthen you and help and uphold you; I will uphold you with my righteous hand (Isaiah 41:10).

Do you have a terrible fear eating away at your faith?

I AM WITH YOU.

Isaiah 41:10

Often in biblical accounts, when all seemed doomed, God stepped in to preserve the promises He made to Abraham and in many ways to the followers of Jesus Christ. Greedy schemers plotted to rob God's appointed people of their divine position and inheritance, appearing to succeed at times. However, there is no record in God's Holy Word of evil ultimately triumphing over good.

"No weapon forged against you will prevail, and you will refute every tongue that accuses you" (Isaiah 54:17).

In Psalm 73, the writer paints a vivid picture of a believer almost slipping in faith while envying the success of the wicked. *"But as for me, my feet had almost slipped; I had nearly lost my foothold"* (v. 2). It is not until verse 17 do we see that he begins to understand the final destiny of the wicked. *"How suddenly are they destroyed, completely swept by terrors"* (v.19). **Finally**, he sees their defeat and awful end. The believer entered into the sanctuary and heard God's Word. God would not allow disobedient, arrogant, evil people to receive more of His glory than His followers. Neither is He slow in keeping His promises. We can consult the record of Abraham, Moses, Jacob, Elijah, Mary, his mother, Peter, and Paul to validate the certainty of God's reward.

An excellent example of good triumphing over evil is seen in II Kings 11:1,2. Jeshosheba, the daughter of King Joram rescued Joash, the heir to the Jewish throne, from the evil hand of Athaliah. She had given the order to slay the entire royal household, killing the last person eligible to inherit the throne of David. God in His infinite wisdom knew that the promise of Jesus' heritage could be fulfilled through just one person. For six years the boy king was hidden for safety before he took his throne and then had Athaliah killed. Jeshosheba's fearlessness in rescuing the future king Joash was wrapped in God's faithfulness. Joash's rescue represented God's help to those who are divinely appointed *and* the triumph over evil.

God further attests to His promises to His people through Isaiah. Isaiah was told to prophesy impending retribution for the people's idolatry and disobedience. Finally, God spoke through Isaiah to give assurance of relief for this doomed people: *"Comfort, comfort my people, says your God. Speak tenderly to Jerusalem, and proclaim to her that her hard service has been completed, that her sin has been paid for, that she has received from the Lord's hand double for all her sins"* (Isaiah 40:1,2). This voice of reconciliation is the pouring out of God's love on a fearful nation—fearful of God's retribution and the enemy's assault. God is now ready and willing to help *His people*.

How long does it usually take you to go to God for a solution to your problem? Why?

Help for Money Matters

The month had more days than dollars. When I realized the condition of the checking account, and the needed income to meet all financial obligations for February, a little uneasiness arose. I had retired recently because the Lord had said it was time to move to another phase in my life. The only problem was a seven hundred a month drop in salary, and an expected new car payment beginning the month after I retired. As usual, I prayed to the Lord and reminded Him of His promises to provide for my needs. Ironically, I had a speaking engagement at a local church in less than a week after my petition.

The occasion was to honor the pastor's wife. When she came before the congregation to make remarks, she presented me with an envelope. The chairperson of the event let her know immediately that an honorarium had been prepared for me. However, the honoree insisted on giving me her token as well.

When I opened the two envelopes at home, I saw the answer to my prayer. The honoree's check was double that of the check from the church. How true is the promise: *"And my God will meet all your needs according to His glorious riches in Christ Jesus"* (Philippians 4:19).

If I had looked to heaven for my help each time, I could have been spiritually strong and bold rather than weak and worn.

A Prayer of Thanksgiving for Being A Refuge

Master, whenever I fear the uncertainties of life, I need to flee to You for reassurance. You are my refuge. In You I trust. Your Word assures me of my deliverance from the plots of Satan to rob me of my peace of mind. He plots but You provide. Hallelujah! You have never allowed anyone or anything to block Your plans. I am so thankful that Your Holy Word is as true today as it was in the time of Isaiah. If You are merciful enough to provide for a backsliding nation, surely You will go the extra mile when we are walking in faith. Thank You for coming to our rescue. I pray in the name of Jesus my Savior. Amen.

I AM YOUR GOD.

Isaiah 41:10

When followers of Christ walk in the path of righteousness and listen attentively, a word or sign is usually enough to propel them to action. An abiding fellowship results in a stimulus-response pattern. The Godhead speaks and the believer obeys. It is our total reliance on Him to see us through the difficult times that sustains us rather than a true absence of fear. Faith in our Almighty God is the launching pad for a leap of faith.

Having to face the unknown is one of the strongest deterrents to obedience. The faithful sometimes will falter when there are untried paths before them. New job. New financial conditions. New travels. New work for the Lord. Dread, indecision and doubt are monsters that loom before us, weakening our knees in the face of these uncertainties. Foolishly, we forget the earlier triumphs, even the most recent times when God strengthened our physical bodies, mental stamina, or faith. When we should have the most confidence, "we lose it."

When we become unglued, unrest and uneasiness abound. We are driven to search out the mysterious and mystical, overlooking the perfect peace offered by God through Jesus Christ. Palm readers, stargazers and humanistic counselors are numerous, and often are made wealthy by answer seekers, sometimes even by those of the household of faith. Some people believe that these sorcerers have the answers to the complexities of life!

There are earnest counselors who can offer logical and well-reasoned advice. However, we often forget their limitations and the absence of infinite spiritual power. These limitations do not keep them from having some degree of expertise. However, they are **not the** Supreme Expert. Unlike the real Expert, God, they are limited in infinite wisdom and final authority.

Isaac's vivid picture of God's work in setting up kingdoms and destroying kingdoms reminded the people of Judah of the awesome power of God. How wonderful to know that He is unconquerable by man. In Him rest divine strength and stability. Out of His wisdom Isaiah spoke to this stiff-necked generation. When God speaks through His Word or through His messenger, we can be assured of the surety of the counsel. Out of His hand comes wise counsel and deliverance. Deliverance came to the nation of Israel, and also for those who are heirs of Abraham through Christ Jesus. Isaiah's reminder to the exiled people is a boost to a doubting and fearful heart: *"You are my people. I am your God."*

How can you distinguish God's voice from the voice of Satan? Have you committed any scriptures to memory on overcoming fear and doubt?

Strength to Endure

When I look back over my life I am awed by how God gave me the strength to endure the odds against me. For some unexplained reason my parents allowed their three oldest children to be raised by my maternal grandparents on a 58-acre farm in Dooly County, Georgia. If you know anything about this part of the country, you know that cotton-picking, pea-picking, corn pulling and a lot of other picking and pulling take place there. The work was hard and long. However, we were blessed with supportive grandparents and an endearing aunt who looked out for our good. Food was plentiful and we lived a high-class poor life.

When we reached high school age, we sometimes had to make the choice of getting up very early in the morning to do our work and be ready to catch the school bus at **7 AM** or miss school for the entire day. We always chose the early work schedule and school for many reasons. Then the bus we had worked so hard to catch often broke down on the way to school, sometimes more than one time in the same day. We then passed three schools on the way to our school. Those were the days of segregation.

All this time I could taste college. Yes, I believe it is not until we can taste our goals in our minds do we fully embrace the fulfillment of them. When I finally made it to college after much picking, and on a wing and a financial need prayer, money became even tighter than before. My granddaddy had lost three of his field hands to city life: one in Florida now with our parents, another cousin in Cincinnati and me in college.

At an early age I learned the power of prayer and the reward of being determined to reach a goal. Whatever the hardship, injustice, barrier or heartache, God often told me through His Word or through other people how to overcome. Even as a child, the Bible was my constant companion, as well as any other book I could get my hand on. The reminders were: "Don't *give up.*" "*Do good works.*" "*Be steadfast.*" "*Do not fret.*"

I cannot say I always followed His advice but I must have abided enough for Him to help me complete college, eventually go to graduate school, raise two daughters after a divorce,—without child support, mind you—who also attended college, and retire after thirty-one years as a public school educator. Foremost, He allowed me to be a servant in His vineyard as a Sunday School teacher, a leader in our Christian Education ministry and eventually a licensed minister. Had I only looked at the odds against me rather than the God for me, perhaps I would have given up at some point in this journey. Because He was looking out for me as I looked up to Him, my needs were met and my goals were achieved.

Fear is a flame. Faith in God through Christ Jesus is a fire extinguisher.

Prayer for Strength in My Hour of Need

Lord, I adore You and magnify Your holy and righteous name. I come in Your presence to be strengthened by Your love and care. Though I am often torn between looking at the barriers at hand and the possibilities ahead, I truly desire to make a clear choice of servitude to You. At times I have been a hypocrite, worshipping both You and the ways of the world. Forgive this awful transgression. Strengthen me to stand firm in my faith and release the fear that is holding me back from complete obedience to You. You are more than enough. Indeed, You have always been more than enough for me. In the name of Jesus who is my example and advocate I pray. Amen.

What is your prayer for strength?

I WILL HELP YOU.

Isaiah 41:10

We must trust completely in the sovereignty and wisdom of God to smooth out our rough places. Submission to His will indicates our perfect faith in an all powerful, all knowing God. We have been made perfect in love through our acceptance in Jesus Christ; therefore, the solutions to our problems are rendered through Christ's intervention. He is at the right hand of God, meditating for us because of His great love for us.

We need to accept His help with open arms, knowing faith brings about perfect solutions. How dare we put our trust in the might of men and in large numbers! Remember: men are not God, and flesh is not spirit. One God is more powerful than ten thousand men. How confident in God we can be when we stop looking at numbers. We then can rely on our one Lord, one faith and one baptism.

"Woe to those who go down to Egypt for help, who rely on horses, who trust in the multitude of their chariots and in the great strength of their horsemen, but do not look to the Holy One of Israel, or seek help from the Lord" (Isaiah 31:1). How desperate Judah was to seek help from the nation that had enslaved their ancestors. How foolish to seek gods of the heathens and not the God of Abraham, Isaac and Jacob. How dare they seek help from the same ones whose chariots and warriors had drowned in the Red Sea! God had mandated their captivity, and only God could release them from bondage.

God's reminder to them through Isaiah was: *"I will help you."* Consultation with God gets the much needed help we request.

Why is God a better problem solver than we are? Why does idol worship or dependence on our enemies bring God's wrath?

"Do not be anxious about anything, but in everything, by prayer and petition, with thanksgiving, present your request to God."   *Philippians 4:6*

Divine Real Estate Agent

During the mid '70's, I desperately wanted to purchase a house. The chance was slim. I was a divorced mother of two with no visible means of support from my ex-husband. Butterflies of fear flapped their wings with dark shadows as I considered one option after the other. Somehow, I decided that surely someone at the bank could help me with my plan. My proposal was for a loan from the bank on my insurance policy. Mind you, I had a term life insurance policy, not a whole life policy with cash value. The vice president listened to my scatterbrain idea and referred me to the mortgage department. All they could do was to tell me the normal procedures to purchase a house.

It was not until I seriously began to petition to the Lord about the purchase that I saw a breakthrough. My mistake became clear, too. I was looking to the bank official because the bank had money. Foremost, I had not taken the time to learn what normal avenues were open to me for securing the money. The breakthrough came once I learned what I needed to know about buying a house AND looked to God who *owned the cattle on a thousand hills*. Here is the proof of God's intervention: I had $300 in my savings account in February, 1979, but when I closed the deal in July, 1979, I had over $2,000 available for the closing.

When I fear making a fool of myself by being obedient to God, I give my enemies the pleasure of laughing at me as I pay the consequences of that disobedience.

Prayer for Spiritual Discernment

Lord, give me wisdom to sense Your presence in all my walks. Give me spiritual eyes and ears to discern if You are leading me to seek help from others. Tell me what I need to do and say, and where I need to go to meet Your approval. Lead me to Your wisdom, Your counsel, and Your comfort. Help me to be receptive to Your leadership, seeking Your kingdom first, thereby ensuring that all the other things will be added unto me. You are my Jehovah Jireh. In the name of Jesus I pray. Amen.

Are you, too, praying for spiritual discernment?

I WILL STRENGTHEN YOU.
Isaiah 41:10

Fear manifests itself more often after a recent triumph. Why? Perhaps our celebration of the victory uses up our spiritual energy. Maybe we forget to keep on our armor to ward off the attacks of Satan. We could have an unbelievable case of spiritual amnesia—forgetting what God has done in the past. Somehow, the trivia becomes major. The senseless takes on meaning in our flight from, and our fight with Satan. It is evident we have forgotten whose we are. Sadly, we forget our foundation as fear takes on a life of its own. We are driven away from the source of our past comfort when we need it most.

Even Elijah, the prophet who defied four hundred and fifty of the prophets of Baal on Mount Carmel, started to fear the threats of Jezebel on his life. His effectiveness had been wrapped up in his prayers to God. He stopped praying and started whining. Was not he the same man who had caused the end of the famine in the home of the woman and her son? Had he not brought the widow's son back to life after he prayed (I Kings 17:7-24)? What had brought about the change? He started to concentrate on what he could lose—his life—and less on what he would gain. Standing bold in the face of death suddenly loomed too large for him. Imagine this senseless fear in light of his awesome Mount Carmel experience. He forgot the commissioner of his work, his prior victories, and His God.

*Was Elijah tired or just **tied to fear**? When was the last time your enemy put you on the run not long after a great faith building experience?*

Going Through the Storm

Several years ago a few students in my high school social studies class had failing averages at the end of the semester. I decided for the first time in my teaching career to allow students to retake the final as well as a few other tests. Sadly, the entire group failed all of the makeup work. Yet one determined mother of one of these students put extreme pressure on me to make extra concessions for her child. She was relentless in her determination to get the failing grade changed, even to appealing the case to the Board of Education. Strangely, the ordeal threw me for a loop. My hair came out. My nerves were on edge. Had not I gone beyond the call of duty to help this student?

One morning during the ordeal I went to school without knowing it had been canceled due to an ice storm. On my way home, I heard a sermon on the radio about enduring a spiritual storm. The unidentified preacher reminded the listeners of God's oversight in times of crises. *"If you are in the storm, God knows you are there. If you are in the storm, He knows why you are there. Therefore, if He knows why you are there, He will come to get you out of the storm."* At that moment I began to glorify God for the solution. What brought an abrupt end to the crisis was one letter with documentation of the student's grades to the Board of Education. When fear and worry were replaced with faith, I became the victor rather than the victim.

I enjoyed victory over the enemy and then forgot what it took to win the next time he showed up.

Prayer for Safety and Security

Heavenly Father, I sense Your presence in the storm and in the face of trials by fire. You have kept me safe and secure even when powerful forces have rallied against me. I feel You holding me in Your hand and lifting me above the storm. Remind me of Your constant, watchful eye when I shake in my boots because of the threats against me. Even in the midst of the storm, remind me to love those who oppress me as Your Son Jesus did. Hear my prayer, O Lord. In the name of Jesus, my Savior, I lift my voice to You. Amen.

What issues of safety and security do you need to pray about?

I WILL UPHOLD YOU.
Isaiah 41:10

We can mock Satan and get away with it when we stand in the power of the Lord, putting aside pride and haughtiness. We need to be extra careful, though. Self-righteous arrogance may impress man sometimes but it does not alter Satan's view of us. He easily sees through our vanity and uses those very weaknesses against us. However, boldness rooted in knowledge of God's ability to uphold us, especially when we stand boldly for Him, is our armor and our shield.

Though the warriors of Assyria outnumbered the warriors of Judah, this imbalance should not have brought fear into the hearts of God's people. Had they not been outnumbered before? Had not they escaped in seven directions when the enemies came in one direction (Deuteronomy 28:7)? Had not the imaginary noise outside the camp of the Arameans frightened that foreign army away (II Kings 7)? Had not God smitten the enemies that put His people in captivity? Did not it happen even after He authorized the seize (Isaiah 34)? Their victory rested in the hands of God, not in *their* military might.

It is God's righteousness that is the measure of our success. It is for His namesake that we are delivered from ourselves and our enemies. He knows that our flesh caves into the lust of the eye and the pride of our heart, causing us to lose the battle. Without His standard of holiness and purity, we would be lost— utterly lost.

When was the last time you were really bold in the Lord? What was the result? What did you do to activate your faith?

Boldness Before Satan

Since my rededication to the Lord, Satan has spent a lot of his time speaking hurried words of foolishness to me. Of course, his purpose has been to get me to act without thinking or praying. I endured these assaults with fear and trembling for years. I was constantly asking God to forgive me for such evil thoughts.

After many lessons and sermons on the defeated fate of Satan, I finally realized that I could talk boldly to him instead of trembling at his will. Now I tell him that he is already defeated, and I am victorious in Christ. I praise the Lord for His greatness when I hear the deceiver's voice. I protect my heart and mind with scriptures.

You know what? He does not show up quite as much. Had God completely blocked Satan's attacks years ago, as I asked, I would not be as mature in Christ as I am now.

I have been adding up the enemies in the camp instead of adding up the promises of God.

Prayer in Remembrance of God's Past Deeds

Lord, help me to remember Your loving kindness and Your protection in times past. Bring Your promises ever before me. Remind me that You stand ready to uphold me in my weakness. Your weakness is always stronger than man's strength, and as Paul told the Corinthian church, Your "foolishness" is always wiser than man's wisdom. Make me a spiritual historian, ever reviewing the record of deeds done for Your people to glorify Your name. In the strong and powerful name of Jesus I pray. Amen.

Are you also guilty of seeking outside help instead of praying to God?

DO NOT BE AFRAID.
Isaiah 41:14

Throughout Christ's ministry, He tried to remove fear from the hearts of the disciples through his lessons on overcoming the evils of the world and, most important, how to be victorious after His impending death. Despite all of the faith building experiences at the wedding at Canaan, on the Mount of Transfiguration and on the roads and byways of Jerusalem, the disciples were still crippled by fear. The most revealing example of their fear was shown by their absence at the time of His trials by the authorities and later His crucifixion. After His resurrection He had to teach the same lesson on overcoming fear to prepare them for their ministry without Him with even more persecution to come.

When Christ told the disciples to fish on the right side of the boat after He appeared to them after the resurrection, He provided them with a means to make a livelihood and a means to live by faith (John 21:1-6). He realized that it is often when our needs are not met that we begin to fear the most, leaving ourselves open to the assault of doubt planted by Satan. Jesus' assurance of the location of the fish and the subsequent heavy catch were intended to alleviate their fears, leading to boldness after His death. 'Fear not" became a daily reminder for the disciples as they faced persecution, perils and sometimes death.

Why did the disciples experience so much fear despite the teachings of Jesus? Do you recognize yourself in them?

A Reminder of His Love

Wearily one night I left the last rehearsal before our church's presentation of *This Is My Beloved Son,* a passion story of the life, death, resurrection and ascension of Jesus Christ. The cast was dragging in movement and spirit. I was wondering how it all was going to turn out the next day. As I ascended the hill of a downtown street, a song came on the radio. The song simply asked how many times did God have to prove that He loved us.

Suddenly, I let go of my fear. It was not my play despite my penmanship and coordination of it. Those were not my people although I had assigned the parts. Had not the Lord brought us through the previous years? The problem was not mine to rehearse. The blessing was mine to wait on if I surrendered it all to Him. I prayed for each staff and cast member by name and went to bed expecting the Lord to do a repeat performance of mercy and grace. What a mighty way He revealed Himself during the presentation and through the manifestation of spiritual gifts after the benediction! He had proved Himself again and again and again!

Heredity and distance limit my eyes. God's eyes are limitless. I think I will use His more.

"Now will I arise," says the Lord. "Now will I be exalted; now I will be lifted up" (Isaiah 33:10).

Prayer for Confidence

God, my Father in heaven, help me to be confident in Your power and Your might. Reduce my reliance on self and increase my reliance on You. You have the power to cast out fear and perfect anything that is imperfect in me. Please bring to my remembrance the stories in the Bible of once cowardly men and women who lost their fear of the enemy and brought victory to the camp. Make me a Deborah prepared for war, an Elijah prepared for worship of the one and only God on Mount Carmel, a Daniel in the lion's den, or a spiritually liberated Paul praying and singing in jail. Speak to me, Lord. Remind me to expect victory because Your name is at stake. In the name of Jesus who conquered death and hell I pray. Amen.

Are you sensing that you need to pray for more boldness for your spiritual warfare?

"Now when Daniel learned that the decree had been published, he went home to his upstairs room where the windows opened toward Jerusalem. Three times a day he got down on his knees and prayed, giving thanks to his God, just as he had done before" (Daniel 6:10).

"Daniel answered, 'O king, live forever! My God sent his angel, and he shut the mouths of the lions. They have not hurt me, because I was found innocent in his sight. Nor have I ever done any wrong before you, O king' " (Daniel 6:21, 22).

THEY WILL BE ASHAMED AND DISGRACED.
Isaiah 41:11

When God selects and anoints a leader or a lineage for leadership, anyone who harms or removes His choice has consequences to pay. They will often be baffled by an unforeseen victory or restoration to power of the "elect." The anticipated triumph by the opponents will end in shame or defeat.

A beautiful example of this scenario is found in Judges 11:2-5: *"And Gilead's wife also bore him sons, and when they were grown up, they drove Jephthah away. 'You are not going to get any inheritance in our family,' they said, 'because you are the son of another woman.'* Some time later, *when the Ammonites made war on Israel* **the elders of Gilead went to get Jephthah from the land of Tob.***"* Imagine their shame in needing the one whom they had robbed of his heritage.

Remember: restoration comes to the righteous. Those who are shunned will be elevated. Stolen inheritances will be reinstated.

You do know that our enemies cannot ultimately win, don't you? Think on this point!

You do know that whatever was taken from you for His namesake will be restored, don't you? Wow!

Can you imagine how Joseph's brother felt when they arrived in Egypt after he had been sold by them to find that he was now their benefactor?

Reclaiming Lost Favor

The following experience did not happen to me; however, I saw it unfold. Several years ago a member of a church was removed from a paid position. Naturally, there was much controversy about legitimacy of the firing. I prayed for the restoration of the relationship and the manifestation of love on both sides of the issue.

Not surprising to me, many years later, she was appointed coordinator of a special project for the person who fired her. I was quite pleased that her dedicated service over the years was acknowledged through this gesture. Satan now had no glory in the final outcome.

God's reputation would be damaged if Satan always won the battle.

Prayer For Defeat of Satan's Plots

Lord, order my footsteps in Your perfect way and lead me to trust in Your deliverance in spite of the obvious obstacles. Keep me ever mindful that my destiny is ordered by You, and even when it appears that I have lost, bring me out in a large place of victory. However, let me demonstrate the love of Christ as I minister to them in their hurt. Let me act as David did when Saul was pursuing him to take his life. Let me not desire to even strike back at my enemies. Clothe me with righteousness and holiness. In Jesus' name and example I pray to You today. Amen.

YOU WILL NOT FIND THEM.
Isaiah 41:12

Even when we are overtaken by fear and run from our enemies, God sometimes calls us out of our "cave" to continue our divinely appointed duties. Despite our disgust, our disillusion or our dread, God will send us forth to anoint, to instruct or even pull someone out of the flames of an earthly hell. The very opponent we thought we could not face, we face boldly through the power of God.

"*There he went into a cave and spent the night. And the word of the Lord came to him: 'What are you doing here, Elijah? The Lord said, 'Go out and stand on the mountain in the presence of the Lord, for the Lord is about to pass by'* " (I Kings 19:9,11).

Why do we hide from our enemies when God has told us to stand boldly in faith? Why did the courageous Elijah hide from Jezebel, a woman not under the covering of God? Had he not experienced the tremendous favor of God in his prayer life? Did not the rain dry up for three and a half years at his request? Did not the drought end three and a half years later also at his request? Had he forgotten the time he had called on the children of Israel to make a clear choice of their allegiance to God and succeeded in defeating over four hundred of Baal's prophets? The problem was quite simple and is still prevalent in faith circle today: He had spiritual amnesia, a dreadful disease of those who walk by faith.

The same God who earlier had delivered him was willing and able to deliver him again. Jezebel was merely a puff of hot air with a facade of power. Elijah should have remembered the promise that our enemies may pursue us but they will either not find us, or they will not find us as vulnerable as expected.

Who are the "Jezebels" in your life?

You ought to be ashamed for fearing such a coward!

My enemies cannot outwit me unless I forget to get instructions from my heavenly headquarters.

"My prayer is not that you take them out of the world but that you protect them from the evil one" (John 17:15).

"I can do everything through him who gives me strength" (Philippians 4:13).

Prayer for Boldness

Lord, I praise You for just being ever wise and eternally wonderful. You have created dwelling places that shelter me in times of trouble; yet, You will not allow me to reside forever in isolation. There is work before me for the cause of Christ, and I must come out to do Your will. Retreating in fear is a reaction to the threats of the world and a sign of spiritual amnesia.

Call me forth to be prosperous or poor, to be multiplied or lessened or honored or despised. For You Lord, even the lowest of these conditions is worth the suffering. Push me. Prompt me to be an instrument of your love, even loving my enemies. Do whatever it takes to get me out of the cave to see Your majesty and might.

Do not take me out of this world, but teach me how to live victoriously in it. It is only when I am victorious here that Satan is revealed as the liar and deceiver that he truly is. Under the blood of Jesus I petition and pray. Amen.

Are you praying in faith for another breakthrough? Did you praise the Lord for the last victory you experienced?

Walking by faith is a sure sign of having on holy war garments.

I WILL TAKE HOLD OF YOUR RIGHT HAND.

ISAIAH 41:13

The real evidence of one's faith comes when there is still joy in the Lord even though nagging and often-minor events arise to overshadow the joy. So often we fail the test because we fret over the trivia, or the "what if," "why not," "if only" or "why me" bellyaches. God promises to hold our hand when we are weak and worn, especially when our fatigue is a result of His work.

So many times I did not feel well or was too tired to think straight. I spent hours counting up all the things I had to do, places to go, and other stresses in my life. Most of the time, my fatigue was a result of working a fulltime job, being a wife, mother and grandmother, teaching Sunday School, attending church meetings, doing outreach, helping the infirm or studying for a sermon. It did not seem fair. If I were working for the Lord, surely I should have been given a break, I thought.

I failed to remember something overheard on the Marilyn Hickey Ministry show. *"When I am too tired to meet my schedule, Jesus is not."*

Have you ever succeeded despite your inadequacies?

Perhaps the work of Jesus and the Holy Spirit according to Romans 8 can help to explain the reason for your success.

Strength for the Extra Mile

Have you ever been asked to do something right after you swore you couldn't do one more thing? Well, I have. My pastor called several years ago to ask if I could teach Bible Study for him the next evening. Of course, I said "yes" but I knew there was no time to really study. I was already in bed for the night, and my schedule was nonstop for the next day. Of course, I wondered why he waited until the last minute to ask. Why did he ask at a time when my schedule was already full and when I was already extremely tired?

When I reviewed my options, I sent up a prayer for help. With only a brief review of the lesson, I stood before the congregation depending on the Lord for inspiration and insight. Many years later, after teaching many more lessons, I still consider it as one of the best lessons I ever presented. Now, I know the answers to the questions I asked to myself at the time. I needed a lesson on the reward of faithfulness. My blessing came from depending on Him **and** having spent many hours in study and communion with Him before this time. Now I know what to do when the sting of fear raises knots in my stomach.

Lord, one day I am going to improve in my reasoning skills. I am going to be able to conclude that when you appoint a work to my hands, you already have a copy of my resume.

Prayer for Perspective

Lord, help me to not "strain at a gnaw and swallow a camel." Keep me from magnifying unimportant details. Lead me away from any attitude of self-defeat or inferiority. Use Your hand to lift me up to experience spiritual victory. Remove fear from my heart and help me to sense the loving pressure of Your hands as I walk this pilgrim's journey. Endow me with the futuristic eyes of the faithful who see the promise when no clear evidence is before them. Give me spiritual x-ray eyes such as You have.

Above all Lord, let love and compassion guide my every step. I ask all of this in the name of Jesus, Your Son and my Lord. Amen.

Should you be praying about getting your priorities in order?

I MYSELF WILL HELP YOU.
Isaiah 41:14

Do you remember the retribution of God when thousands were killed in the wilderness for their rebellion of Moses, God's chosen leader (Numbers 16:1-49)? The root of the rebellion was fear of being stranded in the desert without the creature comforts of Egypt such as a variety of food, houses, cemeteries, and fear that Moses and Aaron had killed some rebels without justification. How could they forget the plagues against the rebellious Egyptians? God had sent a direct command: *"Let my people go."* How could they forget the night of the Passover when God saved them from the death angel? If God protected them then, why would He not protect them now? How could they forget the promises God had kept to the Hebrew nation based on His covenants with Abraham, Isaac and Jacob? They must have feared that the Covenant Maker was like them— unstable, petty, and forgetful.

Have you ever been angry with God or disappointed because He didn't respond the way you had hoped? In light of Psalm 139, was your anger justified?

The Reward of Obedience

One year before I was eligible to retire, the Lord instructed me to change jobs. As department chair, I had only four classes per day. My files were brimming with lesson plans and teaching strategies. My advanced placement history and psychology classes were somewhat of a legend at the school. In other words, I was set to virtually coast until retirement the next year.

The new job at a school for parenting and pregnant girls required me to teach grades 7-12. I had not ever taught any students below the tenth grade. In fact, I had not taught tenth graders in the last seven years or so. Furthermore, different subjects had to be taught during the same period. No normal class situation existed here.

When I accepted the job I made a commitment to work two more years as a matter of personal integrity. The first year was extremely hard. The establishment of a new school is taxing, to say the least. Yet, I was blessed in academic and spiritual growth. It was exciting to be part of a new venture in education, especially one that allowed for shared governance. An added bonus was working with many people who were proud of their faith in Jesus Christ. I like to think I reached some of the girls, and helped them to stay on academic track as well as set personal goals. At least, some of them told me I had.

To top off my reward for obedience, I received an unexpected salary increase because of the lengthened school year. Working two more years with this unanticipated income increase provided me an additional $300 monthly retirement income. Wow! The saying is true: you can depend on the Lord.

My spiritual amnesia can be cured through prayer and faith.

"Because of the Lord's great love we are not consumed, for his compassions never fail. They are new every morning; great is your faithfulness" (Lamentations 3:22, 23).

Prayer for Spiritual Leadership

Father, teach me to honor You and Your plan. Let me not remain in my comfort zone when I fear the untried or unknown. Give me the divine wisdom to trust Your message and messenger. Lead me to the "Promised Land," free of destructive habits, obsessions, greed, lawlessness and aimlessness that lead to sin, crime and self-destruction. Empower me to be a spiritual mover and shaker, doing new things with the same old purpose of pleasing You. I lift up the name of Jesus in prayer. Amen.

"But seek first his kingdom and his righteousness, and all these things will be given to you" (Matthew 6:33).

"In the day of trouble I will call to you, for you will answer" (Psalm 86:7).

YOU WILL THRESH THE MOUNTAINS AND CRUSH THEM TO DUST.
Isaiah 41:15

How many times has God told us exactly what our outcome will be in spiritual warfare? Far more than we can count, I believe. He has laid it out in a simple truth: *"You dear children, are from God and have overcome them, because the one who is in you is greater than the one who is in the world"* (I John 4:4). I can imagine God, the Son and Holy Ghost sadly shaking their head at our refusal to act on these promises.

We forget that God has supernatural power to not only war against our enemies but to **utterly** block their evil intent. We can savor the victory even before it comes. Yet, often this routing of the enemy is based on our obedience to His way. Therefore, our movement from the natural responses of disobedience to the supernatural responses in obedience results in victory on our behalf and great pleasure in us on His behalf.

Have you prayed lately about being delivered from yourself?

The Holy Spirit is cooperating with Jesus to get our message to the Father in a way that is most beneficial to us.

What is the best defense you have ever used against Satan? Have you told anyone else about your strategy?

"The Lord watches over you—the Lord is your shade at your right hand" (Psalm 121: 5).

"Blessed is the man who perseveres under trial, because when he has stood the test, he will receive the crown of life that God has promised to those who love him" (James 1:12).

Lift Up Your Voice and Pray

Many years ago one of my co-workers encouraged me to rush to the principal's office to protest a possible master schedule change, unfairly giving preference to someone else. I had been down this road many, many times before. Instead of rushing to the office, I raised my voice to heaven and quoted scriptures of defeat for those who were making the change. Upon arrival in the office several minutes later, the department head told me that every attempt to rearrange my schedule had failed. You see, I did not have to make any accusation about any injustice on my behalf or give justifications for the initial schedule. God had simply decided which schedule met His criteria for His purposes in my life.

Before all else fails, I can succeed early in my warfare by getting my priority straight: God first and then no need for all else.

"But as for me, I will always have hope; I will praise you more and more."

Psalm 71:14

"Do not be anxious about anything, but in everything, by prayer and petition, with thanksgiving, present your requests to God."

Philippians 4:6

"But you are a shield around me, O Lord; you bestow glory on me and lift up my head."

Psalm 3:3

Prayer for Focus

Lord, so often in the battle or storm You are waiting to hand me the weapon that will defeat the schemes of my enemies. However, to be victorious, my mind must be centered on Your power and might rather than my weaknesses. I must see myself as one delivered unto victory. You desired this achievement for me even to sacrificing of your Son, Jesus Christ. Therefore, I am more than a conqueror through Him. Reduce me and mine in my sight and increase You and Yours in my heart. Following the example of Jesus and in His image, I petition You to hear my prayer and supplication. Amen.

Do you need to pray about focusing more on God's might and less on your minuses and minimal abilities?

"For the Lord God is a sun and shield; the Lord bestows favor and honor; no good thing does He withhold from those whose walk is blameless."

Psalm 84:11

"I lift my eyes to the hills—where does my help come from? My help comes from the Lord, the Maker of heaven and earth."

Psalm 121:1,2

YOU WILL REJOICE IN THE LORD AND THE HOLY ONE.
ISAIAH 41:16

One of the most common fears is fear of opposition. We are reluctant to do as God has commanded because we know some of the obstacles we must face. However, being chosen by God for a particular work does not exempt us from efforts to deter or destroy our works.

The Jews in captivity in Persia found this out when they returned to Jerusalem to rebuild the temple. They had the king's permission, letters of introduction to other rulers on the way, gold and silver from their people, returned temple items taken in the seize by Nebuchadnezzar, and freewill offerings by the Jews. However, the ones who made the trip found great opposition upon their arrival by Sanballat and his followers. The inhabitants who had taken over Jerusalem did everything possible to frighten the builders, and distract them from their designated task.

"Then the peoples around them set out to discourage the people of Judah and make them afraid to go on building. They hired counselors to work against them and frustrate their plans during the entire reign of Cyrus king of Persia and down to the reign of Darius king of Persia" (Ezra 4:4,5).

Would it not seem that their work would be so blessed that no obstacle presented itself? Not so even with the work of the Lord! Seeing their dilemma, the exiles used the resources available to them in the face of their opponents. First, they wrote King Darius about the opposition, and he responded with a letter: *"Let the temple be rebuilt as a place to present sacrifices, and let its foundations be laid.... The expenses of these men are to be fully paid out of the royal treasures...so that the work will not stop"* (Ezra 6:3-8). With the earthly authority is their favor, they continued. However, they did not rely totally on King Darius. The Jews prayed also to the God of their fathers— Abraham, Isaac and Jacob—and continued to build. The temple was restored. Ezra returned with more exiles. The Persians and the Jews praised the Lord for His great work through them.

Despite the opposition our task is to stay focused on the job at hand—not the job of the enemies. If our enemies plot against us, we plot *with* God. If they outnumber us, we buddy up with God. When fear comes over us, we rejoice in the power of the one who has all power. Simple obedience. Simple reliance. **GREAT VICTORY! GREAT JOY!**

I wonder why we are surprised when our enemies attack?

Why is it unreasonable to expect God to keep every obstacle out of our path if we are working on his behalf?

Looking Through the Criticism to Christ

Many years ago I laughed with one of the ministers at church about some recent criticism that I had received. He gave me food for thought when he remarked, *"If you were not doing so much for the Lord, people wouldn't have as much to talk about."* Finally, it dawned on me. I should have expected the criticism and the opposition. Satan was not happy with the bonds being broken and the praises going up to the Lord. He wanted me to feel too insecure to do bigger and better tasks for the Lord. As long as I was doing it for the cause of Christ, I was to count it all joy!!!

I feared my enemy and he defeated me. I faced my enemy, and I defeated him. The latter action took so much less time.

Prayer of Praise

How excellent is Your name in all the earth, O Lord. I praise You for always standing before Your people as a provider and a caretaker. I shouldn't fear any attack on me as I do Your work. The psalm writer assures me that You are a sun and shield, not withholding any good thing if I walk uprightly. Paul says You will give me all sufficiency to do every good work. Standing on the certainty of Your Word, I can look for my forthcoming blessings as well as the imminent defeat of my enemy. I lift up the name of Jesus, my shield and sun. Amen.

> "He grants sleep to those He loves."
> *Psalm 127:2*

> "Never will I leave you; never will I forsake you."
> *Hebrews 13:5*

> "The Lord is my light and my salvation whom shall I fear? The Lord is the stronghold of my life of whom shall I be afraid?"
> *Psalm 27:1*

I WILL NOT FORSAKE THEM.
Isaiah 41: 17

We crucify ourselves between two thieves: regret for yesterday and fear of tomorrow. (Fulton Oursler, American journalist and author, 1893-1952).

Indeed, we do nail ourselves to the crosses of past mistakes and brood over our foolishness. We are haunted mentally by worries of what the future holds. We fret over our errors and panic over the inevitable, the future; foremost, we do not acknowledge God's power to erase our past mistakes through forgiveness of sins. Neither do we recognize the permanent handwriting of His promises. John writes in his epistle a simple requirement for restoration: *"If we confess our sins, he is faithful and just and will forgive us our sins and purify us from all unrighteousness"* (I John 1:9).

Do you ever share how you overcame some of your great mistakes with family and friends?

Moving Past Your Past

For years I lamented over what I thought was a gross mistake on my part. It pricked my heart over and over again. An Israelite in sackcloth and ashes couldn't have been any more repentant. I could not forgive myself. I knew better but I kept beating myself up.

Suddenly one day, I remembered that the decision I thought I had made was not my decision at all. The situation had been taken out of my hands. Another person in authority had told me there was no other option in the matter. I had not committed the sin I had accused myself of for so long.

Being glued to the past had wasted hours of valuable, precious time. My present peace was disturbed. Future dreams were interrupted. The past became an ugly monster in my conscience. Sadly, I failed to realize that old monsters could be laid to rest with prayer and seeking God's evaluation of any of my deeds.

Prayer for Wisdom in Forgiving Self

Lord, You know my past and my future. Grant me the wisdom to release the hurt of the past and savor its teaching, and to anticipate Your blessings henceforth. Remind me to forgive myself as You have done already. Keep me from dwelling on real or supposed shortcomings of my parents, any limitations of my education, the wrongs that were inflicted upon me by family, friends and foes, and let the future loom before me as a call to obedience and ministry. Teach me to use every loss for gain through You and every hurt as a basis for ministering to others. In the precious name of Jesus I pray. Amen.

Have you grown stronger as you have prayed through this devotional? What pattern are you seeing in your life? Have you clearly comprehended that God will help you and strengthen you?

"I call on the lord in my distress, and he answers me."
Psalm 120:1

"For God did not give us a spirit of timidity (fear), but a spirit of power, of love and of self-discipline."
II Timothy 1:7

"So do not worry, saying, 'What shall we eat?' or 'What shall we drink?' or 'What shall we wear?' For the pagans run after all these things, and your heavenly Father knows that you need them."
Matthew 6: 31, 32

I WILL TURN DESERTS INTO POOLS AND DRY LAND INTO SPRINGS OF WATER.
Isaiah 41:18

Often it seems our sources of help have disappeared, and no others are to be found. The mortgage deal fell through. The promised job did not materialize. The person we had depended on failed to follow through on a promise. We lose our hope, and anxiety replaces our optimism. Our emotions then make us feel abandoned by man and God. Satan uses our feelings as piano keys, on which to be played. We repeat the errant ways of forsaking God's counsel as Israel did in Isaiah's time.

Lean Not to Your Understanding

In the memoirs of a booklet based on the life of a strong warrior in our church, Josh Jackson's sister recalled the influence her brother had on her faith. She and her husband were trying to buy a house. A problem came up and the financing did not materialize. Disappointed and disgusted, she told her brother that she was just going to forget about trying to buy the place. However, he turned to her and said, *"O ye of little faith. Trust in the Lord and lean not to your own understanding."* Within a short time, the next attempt was successful. Where there is no water, God can make rivers and oceans. Where there is hopelessness, God cannot only give hope for the moment but can give us eternal assurance.

If we believe His promises, we can endure the wilderness, and see water when there is no cloud, no spring, or no sign of any moisture.

When Paul recorded the Hall of Fame of Faith in Hebrews 11, he reminded us that these men and women saw *"pools in desert places and springs in dry land"* in the absence of such, even to the coming of Christ. They saw the Messiah coming to redeem His people some thousands of years before the manifestation. None lived to see the actual manifestation of the promise, but lived and witnessed to that promise until their death, still never having seen it, yet not thinking it an empty promise. Abraham, Isaac, Jacob, Moses, David, Isaiah, Micah and Malachi never saw Jesus. They knew that their God was able to fulfill His promise regardless of their time frame. The *pool* did not fill up for the nation until the fullness of time of the coming of Christ. Their faith was strong enough to enable them to trust in the wisdom of the Almighty God in the timing of the appearance of the Messiah.

Epilogue

Few people experience the blessed benefit of immediate and decisive obedience to God. Many fail to understand the blessings of submission and servitude to Jesus Christ. Fewer grasp the power available to overcome any obstacle through the presence of the Holy Spirit in us. We face challenges with hesitation. Seemingly, they loom so large before us. Sadly we perceive them as obstacles rather than opportunities to let the glory of God shine. Therefore, we lose so many spiritual battles unnecessarily.

Secondly, the mere thought of isolation by friends and family is enough to frighten some into disobeying God. Others are indecisive, not sure of what or whom to believe. Some people don't feel worthy to speak for God, or stand as a representative of His holiness. Yet, we can overcome the paralysis of fear if we follow the pattern of Isaiah: seek the Lord in the temple, listen to His words, give the revelations of God in the face of rejection, bring reconciliation to the cursed, and stand on faith over and beyond fear.

Isaiah sets the stage for redemption and restoration after a period of fear and frustration: *"If you do away with the yoke of oppression, with the pointing finger and malicious talk, and if you spend yourselves in behalf of the hungry and satisfy the needs of the oppressed, then your light will rise in the darkness, and your night will become like the noonday. The Lord will guide you always; he will satisfy your needs in a sun-scorched land and will strengthen your frame. You will be like a well-watered garden, like a spring whose waters never fail. Your people will rebuild the ancient ruins and will raise up the age-old foundations; you will be called Repairer of Broken Walls, restorer of Street with Dwellings"* (58:9-12). That was His promise to the Hebrew nation and it is mine too because God has now given me the same glorious hope for deliverance through Christ Jesus. If I seek the kingdom of God and its righteousness, all the things necessary for my security and my work in the Lord are ever before me. I must face my future without fear.

Simple Tips for a Faith-Filled Life

Get Into The Word

The message of Isaiah and other scripture writers can be summarized in simple ways to deal with the fear factor. Foremost, read and listen to the Word of God to hear the message of assurance. Trust that message. Meditate on the scriptures to determine what message was given to the particular people at that particular time. Grab the storyline and see how God used that story to teach doctrine, correct or chastise. Digest what the passage is saying to you in light of God's nature.

In many stories, there is a vicious cycle—prosperity, disobedience, consequences of disobedience such as assault by enemies, sickness, captivity, famine or even death, followed by prayer and supplication, and finally God's deliverance. Now search out the stage that is applicable to you. Notice the behaviors to avoid. Claim the promises. Memorize a key verse. Hide the word in your heart. Use it as needed.

Praise Our Heavenly Father

Another way to conquer fear is to praise God for just being God—omnipotent and eternal. Praise Him for the mighty acts of creation of heaven and earth. Learn His different names and attributes. Praise Him for each one. Lift your hands to honor His design of man and man's deliverance after the fall by Adam. Honor Him for the gift of love through Christ Jesus. Praise Him in a full voice for the sacrifices He made for our redemption.

Moses' praise song after the Red Sea crossing brought him blessings in the wilderness for almost forty years. David's many praises in psalms helped to bring him assurance in the "valley of the shadow of death." Paul's praises and prayers opened up prison doors, saved wrecked ships, took the poisonous effects out of the bite of the snake, and fueled a crusade for Christ throughout the known world. Remember this: God will not honor their praises anymore than He will honor ours.

Sadly, we do not praise God as we should. Perhaps because we are self-indulgent, wanting to be like Him: omnipotent. Instead, we should be striving to be obedient. We often resent our subordinate role, and scheme to climb to the high status of God. How? Handle our own problems. Make decisions without consulting the Father and praying through the power of Jesus Christ. Our hearts are stony and filled with pride. The inevitable happens: sin separates us from God, and chaos abounds in our lives. Fear sets in. Desperation abounds more and more. When we come to our senses and lift up the name of the Lord, floodgates open with blessings and the horn of plenty is before us.

Pray With Power and Conviction

A third way to deal with fear is to develop a powerful prayer life. First, learn how we ought to pray. (Matthew 6: 5-15, John 17, Matthew 26:36-42, and Acts 4:24-30.) We can then use prayer as a weapon or a smoothing medicine. It is so powerful that believers ought to be addicted to it. Prayer releases the energy needed for spiritual warfare. It indicates our reliance on the power and authority of God. The more we pray the more victorious we become. A strong prayer life produces spiritual giants. Our work brings glory to His name. We become even more confident because we have repeater's success. We just say, *"Do it again, Lord. Do it again for Your great name sake."*

Speak With Power and Authority

Finally, we must learn to speak with power and authority when confronted by fear, Satan's powerful weapon of defeat. In Luke 9:1 Jesus tells the twelve disciples that they have *"power **and** authority to drive out all demons and to cure diseases."* They were immediately sent out to practice the lesson that had been taught. We go to worship services, Sunday School, Bible study, seminars, workshops and have personal devotion time, but we are often frightened, weak and weary. Our faith is shaky. Our flesh deceives us and our minds are on the things of this world. When we seek the kingdom of God and not this world, God will add all of the spiritual weapons needed for warfare. We should know that we have been made as joint-heirs with Christ. We have the same authority He used when He spoke against His enemies and proclaimed the gospel to His listeners.

The simple truth about fear is that it is of Satan. Furthermore, the simple truth is that it can be overcome. Foremost, the simple truth in overcoming is that we have victory **and** have always had it: first the Jews through the Father, and now us in the latter days through His Son. Sadly, millions have missed this overcoming power. The scholars looked for it in philosophy but a simpleton could have given the answer: Trust and obey. Trust and obey. Trust and obey. Trust and obey. Don't fear. Don't tremble. Don't give up your rightful place of power and authority.

Finally, the simple truth about fear is: we are not to fear because **God will help us, strengthen us, uphold us, never forsake us, deliver us, crush our enemies for us, turn our dry places into pools of water, be our God and claim us as His people.**

If we were to align ourselves perfectly with Christ who is aligned perfectly with God, we could almost have heaven on earth.

Prayer for Serenity

God, grant me the serenity
to accept the things I cannot change,
the courage to change the things I can,
and the wisdom to know the difference.
Living one day at a time,
enjoying one moment at a time;
accepting hardship as a pathway to peace;
taking, as Jesus did,
this sinful world as it is,
not as I would have it;
trusting that You will make all things right
if I surrender to Your will;
so that I may be reasonably happy in this life
and supremely happy with You forever in the next.
Amen.

Reinhold Niebuhr

Prayers

Lord, remind me constantly that I am not to fear. You alone hold the keys to life and death, and heaven and hell. Teach me to give reverence to You in whom there is wisdom and immortality. In Jesus' name I pray. Amen.

Jehovah Jirah, the great provider, I come to you for all of my needs. Spread out your table of plenty and blow your horn of triumph. Cast away my doubts and fears of my inadequacies. Everything I will ever need You have it in abundance just for the asking. Under the blood of Jesus I petition Your care. Amen.

My God and Father, clouds may block the view of the sun and my doubts may block my sense of Your presence, but I am walking by faith. I want to do Your will. Let me not count success as man counts it. Teach me to use Your measuring rod of honest intent and honest actions to judge my ways. You know the depth of my sincerity, and only You can show me my true self. I want to let go and let You be my guide.

Master, let the words of my mouth and the deeds of my body be acceptable to You. Amen.

Lord, honor and majesty belong to You. You are great and greatly to be feared. I am awed by Your majesty when I read Your Word. You bring me a fresh revelation every day through the scriptures. Your strength, compassion and grandeur show up throughout the Bible, and become my comfort in all of my trials. Your greatness becomes my cover and shield. I rest under Your umbrella of protection. In the precious name of Jesus My Savior and Lord I pray. Amen.

Prayer of Surrender

Lord, I surrender to You, the Almighty One. I surrender all of my fears of failure and needless worry. Now I know the simple solution: reliance on the simple truths of Your precious promises. Furthermore, I surrender to the prompting of the Holy Spirit, and accept His visions for my life's work in kingdom building.

You have revealed the plentiful fields for harvest and the lack of workers to reap the crops. Inspire me not only to be a servant in Your vineyard but a model to lead others to do the same. Most of all, empower me as I go forth in Your name and power to be an agent of love and compassion especially to those with the greatest needs, those who know not the way or the truth. In the name of Your Son who conquered death and hell through His blood and made it possible for me to also become a conqueror, I pray. In confidence I petition for help, strength and uplifting. Amen!!! Amen!!!! Amen!!!!!!

About the Author

Mary Taylor Whitfield is a retired educator and founder of Manna of Hope Outreach Ministry, Inc. She has taught Sunday School and coordinated the Christian Education, Productions and Youth ministries at Macedonia Baptist Church, Macon, Georgia. During this time, she has consistently stressed a simple concept for Christian living: trust and obey. Since her call to preach the gospel, she has ministered mainly to women groups and people in crises such as the incarcerated and the distressed.

Though this devotional is her first published work, she has authored and directed several plays including *There Is No Greater Love* and *This Is My Beloved Son*. The latter was a powerful presentation offered as a gift from God to the Macon, Georgia area for nine years, becoming an official event of the nationally recognized Cherry Blossom Festival. People viewed and acclaimed it from around the world. A new play, *What Power! What Glory!*, is on the threshold of production as well as the publication of two additional books. *The Simple Truth About Fear* was gleaned from a compilation of her daily devotions with the Lord and her personal struggle to fight fear with faith.

Trust and Obey!